Going, Going, Gone?

SAVING ANIMALS IN DANGER

BY JOANNE MATTERN

Perfection Learning®

BOOK DESIGN: Jan M. Michalson

ABOUT THE AUTHOR

Joanne Mattern is the author of many books for children. Her favorite topics include animals, biography, and history. She especially likes writing nonfiction because it allows her to bring real people, places, and events to life. "I firmly believe that everything in the world is a story waiting to be told."

Along with writing, Joanne enjoys speaking to school and community groups about the topics in her books. She is also a huge baseball fan and enjoys music and needlework.

Joanne lives in the Hudson Valley of New York State with her husband and young daughter. The family also includes a greyhound and two cats, and "more animals are always welcome!"

IMAGE CREDITS

Cover Image Credits
Left top to bottom: Corbis, Corel, www.arttoday.com, Corel, Corel, www.arttoday.com; right: Corel

Insides Image Credits
p. 3, top to bottom: www.arttoday.com, Corel, www.arttoday.com, Corel, Image Technologies. Corel Professional Photos: pp. 4–5, 10, 12–13, 21, 36, 37, 38–39, 42, 43, 44, 48 bottom, 49, 51, 54. Corbis: pp. 6, 22, 26. www.arttoday.com: pp. 8, 9, 24, 52, 53, 56. Tony Angermayer DGPH, The National Audubon Society Collection/PR: p. 14. © Kevin Schafer/CORBIS: p. 17. © Konrad Wothe/Minden Pictures: p. 18. Jeff Foott: pp. 25, 28, 29. Suzanne L. Collins & Joseph T. Collins, The National Audubon Society Collection/PR: p. 30. Brian E. Beck: pp. 32–33. Digital Stock: p. 34. Image Technologies: pp. 40, 45, 46, 48 top, 50

Contents

Birds. Fish. Insects. Mammals. The world is full of many animals. But some may not be with us much longer.

Some animals are *endangered.* That means they may die out, or become *extinct.* And once an animal family dies out, it's gone forever.

Why are some animals in danger? Some of their *habitats,* or living areas, are disappearing. People destroy the areas by building homes and roads. Habitats disappear when forests are cut down. Pollution also harms habitats.

Sometimes animals move into other animals' areas. The newcomers hunt the animals that were there first. Or they eat all the food.

Poachers are another problem. These people hunt and kill animals. They sell the fur or body parts for money.

Fortunately, a lot can be done to help these animals. Conservation groups work hard to save animals and their habitats.

These groups get laws passed. The laws ban poaching. They also create safe areas, or *preserves*. Hunting is not allowed in these areas. Animals can live safely.

Zoos also work to save animals. Every major world zoo has conservation programs. Some are called Species Survival Plans (SSP).

More than 50 animals have SSPs. Each SSP plans the breeding of chosen animals. In time, their young are returned to the wild.

Many zoos have captive-breeding programs. The zoos mate animals that are in danger. The females bear young. Many animals have more members living in zoos than in the wild!

Zoos also help people understand. They teach why animals are special and important. The more people know about animals, the less they will want to hurt them.

Chapter One

A One-of-a-Kind Animal

The Giant Panda

For years, scientists have argued about giant pandas. Some think pandas belong to the bear family. Others think giant and red pandas are in a group of their own.

Giant pandas live in China. Their favorite food is bamboo. One giant panda can eat 600 stems a day. If there is no bamboo to eat, pandas starve.

In the past, pandas traveled to new bamboo forests if the plants in their areas died. But today, most bamboo forests in China have been cut down. People needed room to live and grow food.

Panda populations grow slowly. Pandas only give birth to one cub at a time. And many cubs don't live to adulthood.

Adult pandas are very large. They grow to 5 feet in length. But the cubs are tiny. They are less than 6 inches long. And they weigh just 3 to 4 ounces. Mother pandas often crush their cubs by accident.

Giant pandas have also been killed. Poachers got a lot of money for these animals. People in Asia used parts of pandas' bodies to make medicine.

Less than 1,000 giant pandas live in China today. So the Chinese want to save these beautiful animals. They have created preserves. There pandas can live safely. And they have plenty of bamboo to eat.

The government has passed laws against killing pandas. In fact, anyone who kills one can be put to death!

Zoos are also trying to save pandas. Over the years, China has sent pairs of pandas to zoos around the world.

Several pairs have given birth to cubs. Scientists spend a lot of time studying them. The more they learn, the better the giant pandas' chances of survival.

Chapter Two

King of the High Mountains

The Snow Leopard

Snow leopards live in the Himalayas of Asia. Not many people live there. So only a few have seen snow leopards in the wild.

These powerful cats climb the mountains to 18,000 feet! They hunt wild sheep and goats.

It's very cold where snow leopards live. But they're prepared. They have wide feet to keep them from sinking in deep snow.

These cats also have beautiful long, thick coats. Their fur keeps them warm. Unfortunately, their coats have put them in danger.

For a long time, people have hunted and trapped snow leopards. Hunters sell the leopard skins. The furs become fancy coats.

Most people living in the Himalayas are poor. A family can earn a lot by selling just one skin.

Snow leopards are still in danger. But there is some good news.

Now scientists are studying these cats in the wild. They want to learn how the cats live. Then they might be able to help the cats survive.

Several zoos have started mating programs. The cats adapt to life there. That makes it hard to send them back into the wild.

There may never be many of these beautiful cats in the wild. But at least some members will survive in the world's zoos.

Chapter Three

Making a Comeback

The Bali Mynah

These colorful little birds live in Indonesia. This is a country in Southeast Asia.

Bali mynahs make their nests in holes in trees. But many of the trees have been cut down. People need the land for farming. They also use trees for firewood.

The birds have another problem. For many years, they were popular pets around the world. Many were captured. Then they were sold to pet stores. By 1990, only 20 of these birds were left in the wild!

Zoos around the world jumped into action. People created programs to save these beautiful birds.

Some of the birds were born in zoos. But they couldn't be released right away. They had no idea how to live in the wild.

These mynahs had lived their whole lives in zoos. They did not have to find food. They did not have to protect themselves. Now people had to teach them these skills.

Some of the birds were sent to the Surabaya Zoo in Indonesia. When they had babies, the chicks were sent to Bali Barat National Park, a preserve.

At Bali Barat, the chicks lived in a protected area. Humans provided berries and other fruit for them. Later, the birds had to find this food on their own.

These birds also had to learn to live together. In the wild, they are very social. They live in large communities. So it was important for them to make friends and form family groups.

The zookeepers watched the birds. They had to be sure the birds were comfortable in their natural environment. They had to know that the birds could find food and survive on their own.

Finally, zookeepers were satisfied. They felt the birds were ready to live on their own. So they put identification

bands on the birds. These bands had tiny computer chips called *transponders.*

Transponders are scanned. They are like the bar codes on things in grocery stores. These would help scientists keep track of the birds. They would also prevent the birds from being sold as pets.

So far, Bali mynahs are doing well. By 1993, there were about 60 birds living in the wild. There were almost 1,000 living in zoos around the world. That's a great start!

Chapter Four

Brazil's Little Treasure

The Golden Lion Tamarin

Golden lion tamarins are small monkeys. They have long, silky, bright orange fur.

These monkeys once lived in millions of acres of forests in Brazil. But over the years, trees were cut down. Farms, ranches, and homes were built on the cleared land. The forests were destroyed.

Golden lion tamarins were captured and sold as pets. By 1970, there were only 200 living in a tiny Brazilian forest.

To make matters worse, only about 70 of the tamarins lived in zoos. And they were in trouble.

Many were sick. Very few babies were born. No one seemed to know how to care for these monkeys. Often the babies died of *rickets.* This is a disease that causes soft, deformed bones.

Zookeepers around the world worked to save the monkeys. They studied the monkeys in the wild. They learned some interesting things.

Zookeepers had been feeding the monkeys only fruit. But in the wild, the monkeys also ate insects and lizards. So zookeepers began feeding the monkeys a more balanced diet.

The zookeepers found out that the monkeys needed a lot of sunshine to stay healthy. Sunshine helps the body make vitamin D. And vitamin D prevents rickets! So the zookeepers made sure the monkeys lived outside, not in dark cages. Soon more baby monkeys were born. And they stayed healthy.

Now the monkeys were healthy and strong. But they still needed a place to live in the wild.

Conservation groups in North America and Brazil worked together. They set aside a place in Brazil. It was called the Poco das Antas Reserve.

Zoos began teaching the monkeys how to survive in the wild. Finally in 1983, the first group of 15 tamarins was sent to Brazil.

At first, the monkeys lived in a large outdoor cage. They had to get used to the sounds, sights, and smells of their new home.

Soon they were set free on the reserve. The monkeys wore tiny transmitters. Scientists could track them and see how they were doing.

By 1993, over 140 golden lion tamarins had been set free. In all, more than 300 of these colorful little monkeys now call the Poco das Antas Reserve home.

Chapter Five

Taking Drastic Measures

The California Condor

In most cases, conservation groups want animals to stay in the wild. It's very rare for animals to be taken out of the wild and put into zoos. But that's just what happened to the California condor.

Condors are North America's largest land birds. They weigh up to 20 pounds. Their wingspans can be up to 10 feet.

These birds are related to vultures. Like vultures, they're scavengers. They use their strong beaks to rip chunks of meat from dead animals.

Over time, many people moved to California. Their ways were not good for condors.

Some birds died when they flew into power lines. Others died from eating dead animals that had been poisoned.

Chemicals sprayed on crops hurt the birds too. These chemicals made their eggshells so thin that they cracked. The chicks inside died.

People finally saw the danger condors faced. But it was almost too late.

Scientists came up with a plan to save these birds. In 1987, they caught all the birds still in the wild. They sent them to the San Diego and Los Angeles Zoos.

Zookeepers formed a plan for the birds. Chicks would be raised in zoos. But they would learn to live in the wild.

Zookeepers faced a special problem. Like other birds, the chicks *imprinted* with the first thing they saw. *Imprinting* means that a bird thinks that the person or animal it first sees is its mother. If a condor imprints with a human, it will not bond with other birds.

The zookeepers made hand puppets that looked like condors. They used the puppets to feed the chicks. The chicks only saw what looked like real condors. This trick helped them learn to live with other birds.

In 1992, the first captive-bred chicks were set free in the wild. Since then, more have been released. By 1999, there were 161 condors in the world. Almost 50 of them live in the wild in California and Arizona. This is considered a huge success.

Chapter Six

At Home on the Range

The Black-Footed Ferret

Once, the prairies of North America were home to thousands of black-footed ferrets. These long, sleek animals belong to the weasel family.

Large groups, or *colonies,* live in underground homes. These are called *burrows.*

Prairie dogs are ferrets' favorite food. But this diet put the ferrets in danger.

Most ranchers and farmers didn't like prairie dogs. These animals dug holes in fields. So they were poisoned.

Black-footed ferrets ate poisoned prairie dogs. Then the poison also killed the ferrets.

By 1986, most scientists thought black-footed ferrets were extinct. Then they got some good news. About 18 were found in Wyoming.

Scientists argued over what to do next. Some wanted to put all the ferrets into zoos. There they would be safe. Others thought they should stay in the wild.

Finally, everyone agreed to capture the ferrets. They were placed in a captive-breeding program. The babies were brought back to the wild when they were 18 months old.

This program is going very well. By 1999, there were 400 ferrets living in zoos. At least 49 more have been set free on government land in Wyoming. New colonies have also been formed in Montana, South Dakota, Arizona, and Colorado.

Scientists hope that one day there will be 1,500 black-footed ferrets living on the prairies.

Chapter Seven

Back from the Dead

The Puerto Rican Crested Toad

Sometimes animals die out when humans bring other animals into an area. The two animal groups often become enemies. That's what happened to Puerto Rican crested toads.

Sugarcane is an important crop in Puerto Rico. But the cane was being damaged by insects.

So people brought marine toads to the island from South America. These large toads ate the insects. But they also ate crested toads.

By 1960, everyone believed that crested toads were extinct.

One day in 1990, a teacher was telling his class how crested toads became extinct. One of the students raised his hand. He said crested toads weren't gone. He had seen them!

The boy proved his story. He brought some crested toads to school.

People heard this story. They decided to save the toads. The key was getting them to mate successfully.

A scientist at the Metro Toronto Zoo in Canada wanted to help save these little animals. He spent hours working in his lab.

Finally, he found the answer. He knew what the toads needed to lay their eggs.

They needed a long dry season. That had to be followed by heavy rains.

Once the toad eggs hatched, scientists studied what conditions were best for them. They also learned what foods the toads needed to survive.

By 1991, there were more crested toads. Some were put back into the wild. But the problems weren't over.

Scientists needed to put transmitters on the toads. These transmitters would track them. Then scientists could make sure they were doing well.

Many large animals wear transmitters on collars. Birds wear metal tags on their wings. But where do you put a transmitter on toads that are only 4 inches long and live near water?

A fashion designer in Toronto made tiny backpacks for the toads. Each backpack held a transmitter!

Puerto Rican crested toads are doing very well. Scientists may not have to continue the program much longer. These little animals are back home in the wild!

Chapter Eight

Giants of the Earth

The African Elephant

African elephants are the largest land animals. They also have the biggest teeth, noses, feet, and ears of any living thing!

In 1992, there were about 600,000 African elephants in the wild. That may sound like a lot. But in 1980, there had been more than one million!

Many elephants were killed by poachers. These hunters sold the tusks for a lot of money.

Elephants' tusks are made of ivory. Jewelry and other decorations are made from it.

In the 1980s, people around the world worked to ban the sale of ivory. In 1989, the president of Kenya

burned 12 tons of ivory. He wanted to show other countries that the ivory trade should be banned.

Finally in 1990, most countries in the world agreed to stop selling ivory. That helped save some elephants.

The Africans hired people to guard the elephants. These people were called *game wardens.*

But there was another danger for elephants. The population of Africa was growing.

Elephants needed a lot of space to live and find food. But people moved into those places.

To solve the problem, several African countries set up preserves. There, these giant animals can live safely and peacefully in the natural world.

Chapter Nine

A Bad Reputation

The Gray Wolf

Gray wolves were once common in the United States and Canada. Large groups, or *packs,* roamed the forests.

Animals in a pack work together to hunt large animals, such as deer and moose. Usually, they only kill very young, very old, or sick animals.

Over the years, more and more people moved into the western and northern parts of North America. They had many problems with wolves.

These people owned ranches. They were angry when wolves killed their cattle and sheep.

Hunters didn't like wolves killing deer. They needed the meat to feed their own families.

Other people were afraid of wolves. They thought wolves would attack and kill them!

Over the years, many wolves were trapped or shot by humans. In time, only a few hundred were left.

During the 1980s, conservation groups worked to bring back the gray wolf. The groups finally made an agreement with the U.S. government. Wolves would be returned to Yellowstone National Park in Wyoming. Wolves had not lived in that park for more than 60 years.

In 1995, about 14 gray wolves were captured in Canada. They were brought to Yellowstone. There they were kept in pens for about two months.

Finally they were released. Later that year, those 14 wolves produced 9 pups. By 1996, about 50 gray wolves were living in Yellowstone National Park.

But not everyone is happy about the wolves' return. Farmers and ranchers still live near the park. They are angry and afraid. They worry that the wolves will leave the park. Then they will kill the cattle and sheep.

So conservation groups have agreed to pay the ranchers for any animals they lose to wolves. The U.S. Fish and Wildlife Service has also agreed to move any wolf that is a danger to humans or their property.

The wolves still have
a rough road ahead
of them. But,
slowly, people
and wolves are
learning to
live together.

Chapter Ten

Too Many or Too Few?

The Tiger

Tigers are the largest cats in the world. They grow to 9 feet in length. A tiger can weigh up to 700 pounds.

There are several different kinds of tigers. They live in many different places in Asia. Bengal tigers live in tropical forests in India and Nepal. Siberian tigers live in cooler mountain forests of China and Russia. Other tigers live in Indonesia.

All tigers need a lot of food. They usually hunt large animals, such as deer, wild cattle, and wild pigs. Sometimes, tigers will kill humans. But this is very rare.

Tigers can live in different habitats. But they still have trouble surviving.

People have cut down many of the trees in Asia. Forests have been destroyed. Tigers have lost their homes.

Tigers are also in danger because of poachers. They kill tigers and sell their beautiful fur. They also sell tigers' body

parts to be made into medicine. It was once thought that tigers would be extinct by the year 2000.

The World Wildlife Fund (WWF) has been working for a long time to save wild tigers. In 1972, the group began "Operation Tiger."

The WWF worked with the Indian government. They set up preserves. There tigers live safely. The WWF has taught people why it is important not to kill tigers.

The WWF worked with the Indian government to save Bengal tigers. Thanks to these people, the number of Bengal tigers doubled between 1972 and 1992. Now about 4,000 tigers live in the wild. That's a big improvement. But it's still far short of the 100,000 tigers that lived in Asia in 1930.

There are also many tigers living in zoos. Tigers mate easily and live for a long time—up to 12 years. In fact, many zoos try to control the tiger population. They have too many!

Even though many tigers live in zoos, it is important to remember that zoos are not their natural habitat. Tigers are wild animals. And that's where they belong—in the wild.

Chapter Eleven

How You Can Help

Saving endangered animals is a big job. No one can do it alone. But one person can make a difference. Here are some ways to help save the animals of the world.

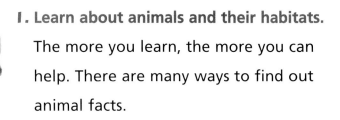

1. **Learn about animals and their habitats.** The more you learn, the more you can help. There are many ways to find out animal facts.

- Read books and magazines.

- Watch TV specials and videos.

- Study CD-ROMs.

- Check out Web sites on the Internet. (Be sure to get your parents' OK before searching the Web!)

- If there is a zoo, an aquarium, or a wildlife preserve in the area, plan to visit.

2. **Set an example.** Live your life with conservation in mind. Your friends, family, and classmates will see what you're doing. Maybe they will want to help too! Here are some ways to set a good example.

- Treat all animals with respect and care. If you have a pet, treat it kindly. Take good care of it. Be kind to other living things, even if you don't like them. For example, instead of squishing a spider, catch it and let it go outside.

- Remember, wild animals are wild. They are not meant to be pets. In fact, they shouldn't have much contact with humans at all. Never try to pet, feed, or play with a wild animal. Both of you could get hurt!

- Keep the environment clean. Litter hurts animals too. Be sure to throw garbage in trash cans, not on the ground. Try to produce less garbage by recycling paper, cans, glass, and other products.

- Join animal-friendly community events. Many communities have "clean-up days." Neighbors pick up litter from roads, parks, or bodies of water. Or maybe a group is collecting money to build a preserve or a park. Try to get involved. And get your family and friends involved too! Or plan your own events. Work with an adult. Then gather your friends to help.

3. **Join a conservation group.** Members work together to save animals all over the world. There's no reason why you can't be one of them! Many organizations help animals. Some have special programs for kids and special "kid zones" on their Web sites. Others publish magazines and books about endangered animals. Check out the organizations below. Choose the one that's right for you.

Canadian Wildlife Federation

2740 Queensview Drive

Ottawa, Ontario K2B 1A2

Canada

Phone: (800) 563-9453

Fax: (613) 721-2902

Email: info@cwf-fcf.org

Web site: http://www.cwf-fcf.org

Defenders of Wildlife

1101 14th Street NW #1400

Washington, DC 20005

Phone: (202) 682-9400

Email: info@defenders.org

Web site: http://www.defenders.org

The Fund for Animals

200 West 57th Street

New York, NY 10019

Phone: (212) 246-2096

Fax: (212) 246-2633

Email: fundinfo@fund.org

Web site: http://www.fund.org

The Humane Society of the United States

2100 L Street NW

Washington, DC 20037

Web site: http://www.hsus.org

National Wildlife Federation

8925 Leesburg Pike

Vienna, VA 22184

Phone: (703) 790-4000

Web site: http://nwf.org

Wildlife Conservation Society

2300 Southern Blvd.

Bronx, NY 10460

Phone: (718) 220-5111

Web site: http://www.wcs.org

World Wildlife Fund

1250 24th Street NW

P.O. Box 97180

Washington, DC 20077-7180

Phone: (800) 225-5993

Web site: http://www.worldwildlife.org

Note: Many organizations charge a membership fee to join or to receive their magazines. If you don't have the money to join, maybe you could ask for a membership for a birthday present or another holiday or event. Talk to your parents about joining as a family.